50 15-Minute Gourmet Recipes for Home

By: Kelly Johnson

Table of Contents

- Grilled Balsamic Chicken with Strawberry Salsa
- Seared Scallops with Lemon Brown Butter
- Caprese Avocado Toast with Balsamic Glaze
- Blackened Salmon with Mango Salsa
- Garlic Butter Shrimp and Asparagus Stir-Fry
- Lemon Herb Quinoa Salad with Roasted Vegetables
- Pan-Seared Tofu with Ginger Soy Glaze
- Pesto Zucchini Noodles with Cherry Tomatoes
- Thai Basil Beef Stir-Fry
- Fig and Goat Cheese Crostini with Honey Drizzle
- Quick and Easy Lobster Tail with Garlic Butter
- Mediterranean Chickpea Salad with Feta
- Teriyaki Glazed Salmon with Sesame Seeds
- Herb-Marinated Grilled Portobello Mushrooms
- Spinach and Artichoke Stuffed Chicken Breast
- Lemon Garlic Shrimp Pasta with Cherry Tomatoes
- Avocado Lime Cilantro Rice Bowl
- Pan-Seared Gnocchi with Brown Butter and Sage
- Harissa Grilled Eggplant with Yogurt Sauce
- Cucumber Dill Greek Yogurt Dip with Pita Chips
- Hoisin Glazed Tofu Stir-Fry
- Mango Avocado Salsa with Grilled Chicken
- Smoked Salmon and Cream Cheese Cucumber Bites
- Quick and Easy Beef and Broccoli
- Lemon Thyme Grilled Swordfish
- Quinoa Salad with Roasted Vegetables and Feta
- Spicy Garlic Butter Shrimp Tacos
- Caprese Stuffed Portobello Mushrooms
- Baked Brie with Honey and Walnuts
- Mediterranean Tuna Salad Wraps
- Pistachio-Crusted Dijon Salmon
- Pomegranate and Goat Cheese Spinach Salad
- Basil Pesto Pasta with Cherry Tomatoes
- Lemon Rosemary Grilled Chicken Skewers
- Shrimp and Avocado Ceviche

- Prosciutto-Wrapped Asparagus Bundles
- Sesame Ginger Quinoa Bowl with Vegetables
- Grilled Halloumi and Watermelon Skewers
- Lemon Butter Cod with Garlic Parmesan Asparagus
- Balsamic Glazed Brussels Sprouts with Bacon
- Tomato Basil Mozzarella Stacks
- Quick and Easy Shrimp Scampi
- Spinach and Feta Stuffed Chicken Breast
- 15-Minute Beef and Vegetable Stir-Fry
- Mango Coconut Chia Pudding Parfait
- Sriracha Lime Grilled Shrimp Skewers
- Caprese Couscous Salad with Balsamic Vinaigrette
- Grilled Teriyaki Tofu and Pineapple Skewers
- Lemon Dill Salmon Salad Lettuce Wraps
- Mediterranean Hummus and Veggie Wrap

Grilled Balsamic Chicken with Strawberry Salsa

Ingredients:

For the Balsamic Chicken:

- 4 boneless, skinless chicken breasts
- 1/4 cup balsamic vinegar
- 2 tablespoons olive oil
- 2 cloves garlic, minced
- 1 teaspoon dried oregano
- Salt and black pepper, to taste

For the Strawberry Salsa:

- 1 cup fresh strawberries, diced
- 1/2 red onion, finely chopped
- 1/4 cup fresh basil, chopped
- 1 tablespoon balsamic vinegar
- 1 tablespoon olive oil
- Salt and black pepper, to taste

Instructions:

1. Marinate the Chicken:

- In a bowl, whisk together balsamic vinegar, olive oil, minced garlic, dried oregano, salt, and black pepper.
- Place the chicken breasts in a resealable plastic bag or shallow dish and pour the marinade over them.
- Seal the bag or cover the dish and refrigerate for at least 30 minutes to allow the flavors to infuse.

2. Preheat the Grill:

- Preheat your grill to medium-high heat.

3. Grill the Chicken:

- Remove the chicken from the marinade and discard the marinade.
- Grill the chicken breasts for about 6-8 minutes per side or until fully cooked, with grill marks and juices running clear.
- Ensure the internal temperature of the chicken reaches 165°F (74°C).

4. Prepare the Strawberry Salsa:

- In a bowl, combine diced strawberries, chopped red onion, fresh basil, balsamic vinegar, olive oil, salt, and black pepper.
- Toss the ingredients together until well mixed.

5. Serve:

- Plate the grilled balsamic chicken and top each piece with a generous spoonful of strawberry salsa.

6. Garnish and Enjoy:

- Garnish with additional fresh basil, if desired.
- Serve the Grilled Balsamic Chicken with Strawberry Salsa immediately.

This dish is a perfect blend of savory and sweet, making it a refreshing and satisfying option for a light and tasty meal. Enjoy!

Seared Scallops with Lemon Brown Butter

Ingredients:

- 1 pound large sea scallops, patted dry
- Salt and black pepper, to taste
- 2 tablespoons olive oil
- 4 tablespoons unsalted butter
- 2 tablespoons fresh lemon juice
- Zest of 1 lemon
- 2 tablespoons chopped fresh parsley (for garnish)
- Lemon wedges (for serving)

Instructions:

1. Prepare Scallops:

- Ensure the scallops are dry by patting them with paper towels.
- Season both sides of the scallops with salt and black pepper.

2. Sear the Scallops:

- Heat olive oil in a large skillet over medium-high heat until hot but not smoking.
- Add the scallops to the skillet, making sure they are not overcrowded. Leave space between each scallop for proper searing.
- Sear the scallops for 1.5 to 2 minutes per side or until they develop a golden-brown crust. Be careful not to overcook; scallops should be opaque in the center.

3. Make the Lemon Brown Butter:

- In the same skillet, reduce the heat to medium, and add the butter.
- Allow the butter to melt and continue cooking until it starts to turn a light brown color. Swirl the pan occasionally to prevent burning.
- Once the butter is browned and has a nutty aroma, remove the skillet from heat.

4. Finish with Lemon:

- Add fresh lemon juice and lemon zest to the brown butter. Stir to combine.

5. Serve:

- Arrange the seared scallops on a serving platter.
- Drizzle the lemon brown butter sauce over the scallops.

6. Garnish and Enjoy:

- Garnish with chopped fresh parsley.
- Serve the Seared Scallops with Lemon Brown Butter immediately, with lemon wedges on the side for extra flavor.

This dish is perfect for a special occasion or when you want to treat yourself to a restaurant-quality meal at home. Enjoy the delicious combination of seared scallops and the rich, nutty aroma of lemon brown butter!

Caprese Avocado Toast with Balsamic Glaze

Ingredients:

- 2 ripe avocados
- 4 slices whole-grain or artisan bread, toasted
- 1 cup cherry tomatoes, halved
- 1 cup fresh mozzarella, sliced
- Fresh basil leaves, for garnish
- Balsamic glaze, for drizzling
- Extra virgin olive oil, for drizzling
- Salt and black pepper, to taste

Instructions:

1. Prepare Avocado:

- Slice the avocados and mash them lightly with a fork in a bowl.
- Season the mashed avocados with salt and black pepper to taste.

2. Toast the Bread:

- Toast the slices of bread until golden and crispy.

3. Assemble the Avocado Toast:

- Spread a generous layer of mashed avocado onto each slice of toasted bread.

4. Top with Caprese Ingredients:

- Arrange halved cherry tomatoes and slices of fresh mozzarella on top of the mashed avocado.

5. Garnish:

- Garnish each toast with fresh basil leaves.

6. Drizzle with Balsamic Glaze and Olive Oil:

- Drizzle balsamic glaze and extra virgin olive oil over each avocado toast.

7. Season:

- Sprinkle a pinch of salt and black pepper over the assembled toasts.

8. Serve:

- Serve the Caprese Avocado Toast with Balsamic Glaze immediately, while the toast is still warm.

This Caprese Avocado Toast is a perfect balance of creamy avocado, juicy tomatoes, fresh mozzarella, and the sweet and tangy notes of balsamic glaze. It makes for a delicious and visually appealing breakfast or brunch option. Enjoy!

Blackened Salmon with Mango Salsa

Ingredients:

For the Blackened Salmon:

- 4 salmon fillets
- 2 tablespoons Cajun seasoning
- 1 teaspoon paprika
- 1 teaspoon dried thyme
- 1 teaspoon garlic powder
- 1 teaspoon onion powder
- Salt and black pepper, to taste
- 2 tablespoons olive oil

For the Mango Salsa:

- 1 large ripe mango, peeled, pitted, and diced
- 1/2 red onion, finely chopped
- 1 red bell pepper, diced
- 1 jalapeño, seeded and minced
- Juice of 1 lime
- 2 tablespoons fresh cilantro, chopped
- Salt and black pepper, to taste

Instructions:

1. Prepare the Mango Salsa:

- In a bowl, combine diced mango, chopped red onion, diced red bell pepper, minced jalapeño, lime juice, and chopped cilantro.
- Season the salsa with salt and black pepper to taste.
- Refrigerate the salsa while you prepare the salmon.

2. Blacken the Salmon:

- In a small bowl, mix Cajun seasoning, paprika, dried thyme, garlic powder, onion powder, salt, and black pepper.
- Pat the salmon fillets dry with paper towels.
- Rub each fillet with the spice mixture, ensuring it's well coated on all sides.

3. Cook the Salmon:

- Heat olive oil in a skillet over medium-high heat.
- Once the oil is hot, add the salmon fillets to the skillet.
- Cook the salmon for about 3-4 minutes per side or until the edges are crispy, and the salmon is cooked through and flakes easily.

4. Serve:

- Place the blackened salmon fillets on a serving platter.

5. Top with Mango Salsa:

- Spoon the prepared mango salsa over the blackened salmon fillets.

6. Garnish:

- Garnish with additional cilantro if desired.

7. Serve:

- Serve the Blackened Salmon with Mango Salsa immediately, with additional lime wedges on the side if desired.

This dish brings together the spicy kick of blackened salmon and the refreshing sweetness of mango salsa, creating a perfect balance of flavors. It's a delightful and colorful meal that's sure to impress!

Garlic Butter Shrimp and Asparagus Stir-Fry

Ingredients:

- 1 pound large shrimp, peeled and deveined
- 1 bunch asparagus, trimmed and cut into bite-sized pieces
- 4 tablespoons unsalted butter
- 4 cloves garlic, minced
- 1 tablespoon soy sauce
- 1 tablespoon oyster sauce
- 1 teaspoon fish sauce (optional)
- 1 teaspoon sesame oil
- Red pepper flakes (optional, for heat)
- Salt and black pepper, to taste
- Fresh parsley or cilantro, chopped (for garnish)
- Cooked rice or noodles, for serving

Instructions:

1. Prepare Shrimp and Asparagus:

- Pat the shrimp dry with paper towels.
- Trim the asparagus and cut it into bite-sized pieces.

2. Cook Shrimp:

- In a large skillet or wok, melt 2 tablespoons of butter over medium-high heat.
- Add the shrimp to the skillet and cook for 1-2 minutes per side or until they start to turn pink. Remove the shrimp from the skillet and set aside.

3. Stir-Fry Asparagus:

- In the same skillet, add the remaining 2 tablespoons of butter.
- Add minced garlic and stir-fry for about 30 seconds until fragrant.
- Add the asparagus and stir-fry for 3-4 minutes until they are crisp-tender.

4. Combine Shrimp and Asparagus:

- Return the cooked shrimp to the skillet with the asparagus.

5. Prepare Sauce:

- In a small bowl, mix soy sauce, oyster sauce, fish sauce (if using), sesame oil, red pepper flakes (if using), salt, and black pepper.

6. Add Sauce to Skillet:

- Pour the sauce over the shrimp and asparagus.
- Stir-fry for an additional 1-2 minutes, ensuring everything is well coated and heated through.

7. Garnish and Serve:

- Garnish the Garlic Butter Shrimp and Asparagus Stir-Fry with chopped fresh parsley or cilantro.
- Serve over cooked rice or noodles.

This Garlic Butter Shrimp and Asparagus Stir-Fry is a delicious and speedy option for a weeknight dinner. The combination of garlic butter and savory sauces enhances the natural flavors of the shrimp and asparagus. Enjoy your flavorful stir-fry!

Lemon Herb Quinoa Salad with Roasted Vegetables

Ingredients:

For the Quinoa Salad:

- 1 cup quinoa, rinsed
- 2 cups water or vegetable broth
- 1 cup cherry tomatoes, halved
- 1 zucchini, diced
- 1 red bell pepper, diced
- 1 yellow bell pepper, diced
- 1 red onion, thinly sliced
- 2 tablespoons olive oil
- Salt and black pepper, to taste
- Fresh parsley or basil, chopped (for garnish)

For the Lemon Herb Dressing:

- 1/4 cup olive oil
- 2 tablespoons fresh lemon juice
- 1 teaspoon Dijon mustard
- 1 clove garlic, minced
- 1 teaspoon dried oregano
- 1 teaspoon dried thyme
- Salt and black pepper, to taste

Instructions:

1. Roast Vegetables:

- Preheat the oven to 400°F (200°C).
- In a large bowl, toss the cherry tomatoes, diced zucchini, diced red and yellow bell peppers, and thinly sliced red onion with olive oil, salt, and black pepper.
- Spread the vegetables on a baking sheet in a single layer.
- Roast in the preheated oven for about 20-25 minutes or until the vegetables are tender and slightly caramelized, stirring halfway through.

2. Cook Quinoa:

- In a medium saucepan, combine quinoa and water or vegetable broth.
- Bring to a boil, then reduce the heat to low, cover, and simmer for 15-20 minutes or until the quinoa is cooked and water is absorbed.
- Fluff the quinoa with a fork and let it cool.

3. Prepare Lemon Herb Dressing:

- In a small bowl, whisk together olive oil, fresh lemon juice, Dijon mustard, minced garlic, dried oregano, dried thyme, salt, and black pepper.

4. Assemble the Salad:

- In a large bowl, combine the cooked quinoa and roasted vegetables.
- Drizzle the lemon herb dressing over the salad and toss to coat evenly.

5. Garnish and Serve:

- Garnish the Lemon Herb Quinoa Salad with Roasted Vegetables with chopped fresh parsley or basil.
- Serve the salad warm or at room temperature.

This Lemon Herb Quinoa Salad with Roasted Vegetables is not only delicious but also packed with wholesome ingredients. It's perfect as a side dish or a light main course for a nutritious and satisfying meal. Enjoy!

Pan-Seared Tofu with Ginger Soy Glaze

Ingredients:

For the Pan-Seared Tofu:

- 1 block extra-firm tofu, pressed and cut into slices
- 2 tablespoons soy sauce
- 1 tablespoon cornstarch
- 2 tablespoons vegetable oil

For the Ginger Soy Glaze:

- 2 tablespoons soy sauce
- 1 tablespoon rice vinegar
- 1 tablespoon maple syrup or agave nectar
- 1 tablespoon fresh ginger, grated
- 1 clove garlic, minced
- 1 teaspoon sesame oil
- Sesame seeds and green onions for garnish (optional)

Instructions:

1. Prepare the Tofu:

- Press the tofu to remove excess water. Cut the pressed tofu into slices, about 1/2-inch thick.
- In a shallow bowl, mix soy sauce and cornstarch to create a marinade.
- Dip each tofu slice into the marinade, ensuring both sides are coated.

2. Pan-Seared Tofu:

- Heat vegetable oil in a non-stick skillet over medium-high heat.
- Add the tofu slices to the hot skillet and sear for 2-3 minutes per side or until golden brown and crispy.
- Remove the tofu from the skillet and set aside.

3. Prepare Ginger Soy Glaze:

- In a small saucepan, combine soy sauce, rice vinegar, maple syrup or agave nectar, grated ginger, minced garlic, and sesame oil.
- Cook over medium heat, stirring continuously, until the glaze thickens slightly (about 2-3 minutes).

4. Coat Tofu with Glaze:

- Pour the ginger soy glaze over the pan-seared tofu slices, ensuring they are well coated.

5. Garnish and Serve:

- Garnish with sesame seeds and chopped green onions if desired.
- Serve the Pan-Seared Tofu with Ginger Soy Glaze over rice or noodles.

Enjoy this Pan-Seared Tofu with Ginger Soy Glaze as a delicious and satisfying vegetarian option. The combination of crispy tofu and the savory-sweet glaze creates a delightful harmony of flavors!

Pesto Zucchini Noodles with Cherry Tomatoes

Ingredients:

For the Pesto Sauce:

- 2 cups fresh basil leaves, packed
- 1/2 cup grated Parmesan cheese
- 1/3 cup pine nuts
- 2 cloves garlic, peeled
- 1/2 cup extra-virgin olive oil
- Salt and black pepper, to taste

For the Zucchini Noodles:

- 4 medium-sized zucchini, spiralized into noodles
- 1 cup cherry tomatoes, halved
- Grated Parmesan cheese, for garnish
- Pine nuts, for garnish (optional)
- Fresh basil leaves, for garnish

Instructions:

1. Prepare Pesto Sauce:

- In a food processor, combine fresh basil, grated Parmesan cheese, pine nuts, and garlic.
- Pulse until the ingredients are finely chopped.
- With the food processor running, slowly drizzle in the olive oil until the pesto reaches a smooth consistency.
- Season with salt and black pepper to taste. Set aside.

2. Spiralize Zucchini:

- Use a spiralizer to turn the zucchini into noodles.

3. Cook Zucchini Noodles:

- In a large skillet, heat a bit of olive oil over medium heat.
- Add the zucchini noodles and toss for 2-3 minutes, just until they are slightly softened. Be careful not to overcook; you want them to retain a bit of crunch.

4. Toss with Pesto:

- Add the prepared pesto sauce to the skillet with the zucchini noodles.
- Toss until the noodles are evenly coated with the pesto.

5. Add Cherry Tomatoes:

- Gently fold in the halved cherry tomatoes, allowing them to warm through but not fully cook.

6. Garnish:

- Garnish the Pesto Zucchini Noodles with Cherry Tomatoes with grated Parmesan cheese, pine nuts (if using), and fresh basil leaves.

7. Serve:

- Serve the dish immediately, either as a light main course or as a side dish.

This Pesto Zucchini Noodles with Cherry Tomatoes is a delicious and nutritious alternative to traditional pasta. It's perfect for a quick and light meal, especially during the warmer months when fresh produce is abundant. Enjoy!

Thai Basil Beef Stir-Fry

Ingredients:

For the Stir-Fry:

- 1 pound flank steak or sirloin, thinly sliced against the grain
- 2 tablespoons vegetable oil
- 4 cloves garlic, minced
- 1 red chili, sliced (adjust to your spice preference)
- 1 bell pepper, thinly sliced
- 1 onion, thinly sliced
- 1 cup Thai basil leaves, loosely packed

For the Sauce:

- 3 tablespoons soy sauce
- 2 tablespoons oyster sauce
- 1 tablespoon fish sauce
- 1 tablespoon sugar
- 1 tablespoon water

Instructions:

1. Prepare the Sauce:

- In a small bowl, whisk together soy sauce, oyster sauce, fish sauce, sugar, and water. Set aside.

2. Stir-Fry Beef:

- Heat vegetable oil in a wok or large skillet over high heat.
- Add minced garlic and sliced red chili, stir-frying for about 30 seconds until fragrant.

3. Cook Beef:

- Add the thinly sliced beef to the wok or skillet.
- Stir-fry the beef for 2-3 minutes until it's browned and cooked through.

4. Add Vegetables:

- Add sliced bell pepper and onion to the wok, continuing to stir-fry for an additional 2-3 minutes until the vegetables are tender-crisp.

5. Incorporate Sauce:

- Pour the prepared sauce over the beef and vegetables.
- Toss everything together to ensure that the beef and vegetables are well-coated with the sauce.

6. Add Thai Basil:

- Add Thai basil leaves to the wok or skillet.
- Stir-fry for an additional 1-2 minutes until the basil wilts and releases its aromatic flavor.

7. Serve:

- Remove the Thai Basil Beef Stir-Fry from heat.
- Serve immediately over steamed rice.

8. Garnish (Optional):

- Garnish with additional fresh Thai basil leaves and sliced red chili if desired.

Enjoy your Thai Basil Beef Stir-Fry, a delicious and quick dish that showcases the bold and aromatic flavors of Thai cuisine!

Fig and Goat Cheese Crostini with Honey Drizzle

Ingredients:

- Baguette, sliced into 1/2-inch thick rounds
- Fresh figs, ripe and sliced
- Goat cheese
- Honey, for drizzling
- Fresh thyme leaves (optional, for garnish)

Instructions:

1. Toast the Baguette:

   - Preheat the oven to 375°F (190°C).
   - Arrange the baguette slices on a baking sheet.
   - Toast in the oven for about 5-7 minutes or until the edges are golden and crispy.

2. Spread Goat Cheese:

   - Allow the toasted baguette slices to cool slightly.
   - Spread a layer of goat cheese onto each slice.

3. Add Sliced Figs:

   - Place a few slices of ripe figs on top of the goat cheese layer.

4. Drizzle with Honey:

   - Drizzle honey over each crostini, ensuring a sweet contrast to the savory goat cheese and the natural sweetness of the figs.

5. Garnish (Optional):

   - Optionally, garnish each crostini with fresh thyme leaves for an extra layer of flavor and visual appeal.

6. Serve:

   - Arrange the Fig and Goat Cheese Crostini on a serving platter.

This appetizer is a perfect balance of textures and flavors, making it an elegant and easy-to-assemble option for entertaining guests or enjoying a special snack. The combination of creamy goat cheese, juicy figs, and sweet honey creates a palate-pleasing treat. Enjoy!

Quick and Easy Lobster Tail with Garlic Butter

Ingredients:

- 2 lobster tails, thawed if frozen
- 4 tablespoons unsalted butter, melted
- 4 cloves garlic, minced
- 1 tablespoon fresh parsley, chopped
- Salt and black pepper, to taste
- Lemon wedges, for serving

Instructions:

1. Prepare Lobster Tails:

    - Preheat the oven to 425°F (220°C).
    - Use kitchen shears to cut through the top shell of each lobster tail, stopping at the base of the tail.

2. Butterfly Lobster Tails:

    - Gently pull the lobster meat upward and rest it on top of the shells, creating a "butterfly" shape.

3. Make Garlic Butter:

    - In a small bowl, combine melted butter, minced garlic, chopped parsley, salt, and black pepper. Mix well.

4. Brush with Garlic Butter:

    - Place the lobster tails on a baking sheet.
    - Brush the lobster meat with the prepared garlic butter mixture, ensuring even coverage.

5. Bake:

- Bake the lobster tails in the preheated oven for about 12-15 minutes or until the lobster meat is opaque and cooked through.

6. Broil (Optional):

- If desired, you can broil the lobster tails for an additional 1-2 minutes to give them a golden finish. Keep a close eye to prevent burning.

7. Serve:

- Remove the lobster tails from the oven.
- Serve the lobster tails with lemon wedges on the side for squeezing over the meat.

8. Garnish (Optional):

- Garnish with additional chopped parsley for a fresh touch.

This quick and easy lobster tail with garlic butter is a fantastic way to enjoy the succulent and delicate flavor of lobster. It's perfect for special occasions or when you want to treat yourself to a luxurious meal at home. Enjoy!

Mediterranean Chickpea Salad with Feta

Ingredients:

For the Salad:

- 2 cans (15 ounces each) chickpeas, drained and rinsed
- 1 cucumber, diced
- 1 cup cherry tomatoes, halved
- 1/2 red onion, finely chopped
- 1/2 cup Kalamata olives, pitted and sliced
- 1/2 cup crumbled feta cheese
- 1/4 cup fresh parsley, chopped
- 1/4 cup fresh mint, chopped

For the Dressing:

- 1/4 cup extra-virgin olive oil
- 2 tablespoons red wine vinegar
- 1 clove garlic, minced
- 1 teaspoon dried oregano
- Salt and black pepper, to taste

Instructions:

1. Prepare Chickpeas:

- Drain and rinse the chickpeas thoroughly.

2. Make the Dressing:

- In a small bowl, whisk together the olive oil, red wine vinegar, minced garlic, dried oregano, salt, and black pepper to create the dressing. Set aside.

3. Assemble the Salad:

- In a large mixing bowl, combine the chickpeas, diced cucumber, cherry tomatoes, chopped red onion, sliced Kalamata olives, crumbled feta cheese, fresh parsley, and fresh mint.

4. Dress the Salad:

- Pour the dressing over the salad.

5. Toss and Chill:

- Gently toss the salad until all ingredients are well coated with the dressing.
- Refrigerate the salad for at least 30 minutes to allow the flavors to meld.

6. Serve:

- Before serving, give the salad a final toss.
- Garnish with additional fresh herbs if desired.

This Mediterranean Chickpea Salad with Feta is a perfect side dish or a light and satisfying main course. It's packed with wholesome ingredients and the bold flavors of the Mediterranean. Enjoy the combination of chickpeas, feta, and vibrant vegetables!

Teriyaki Glazed Salmon with Sesame Seeds

Ingredients:

- 4 salmon fillets
- 1/4 cup soy sauce
- 2 tablespoons mirin (sweet rice wine)
- 2 tablespoons sake (or dry white wine)
- 2 tablespoons brown sugar
- 1 tablespoon honey
- 1 tablespoon sesame oil
- 2 cloves garlic, minced
- 1 teaspoon grated ginger
- 1 tablespoon cornstarch (optional, for thickening)
- Sesame seeds, toasted, for garnish
- Green onions, chopped, for garnish (optional)
- Cooked white or brown rice, for serving

Instructions:

1. Prepare Teriyaki Glaze:

- In a small saucepan, combine soy sauce, mirin, sake, brown sugar, honey, sesame oil, minced garlic, and grated ginger.
- Bring the mixture to a simmer over medium heat, stirring to dissolve the sugar.
- Optional: In a small bowl, mix cornstarch with a little water to create a slurry. Add the slurry to the sauce to thicken it. Stir well and simmer until the sauce reaches the desired thickness.

2. Marinate Salmon:

- Place the salmon fillets in a shallow dish or a resealable plastic bag.
- Pour half of the teriyaki glaze over the salmon, ensuring the fillets are well coated.
- Allow the salmon to marinate for at least 15-30 minutes in the refrigerator.

3. Preheat Oven:

- Preheat the oven to 400°F (200°C).

4. Bake Salmon:

- Place the marinated salmon fillets on a baking sheet lined with parchment paper.
- Bake in the preheated oven for 12-15 minutes or until the salmon is cooked through and flakes easily with a fork.

5. Glaze Salmon:

- Brush the baked salmon with the remaining teriyaki glaze during the last few minutes of cooking.

6. Garnish:

- Sprinkle toasted sesame seeds and chopped green onions over the glazed salmon.

7. Serve:

- Serve the Teriyaki Glazed Salmon with Sesame Seeds over cooked rice.

This Teriyaki Glazed Salmon with Sesame Seeds is a delicious and satisfying dish with a perfect balance of sweet, savory, and nutty flavors. Enjoy your flavorful salmon dinner!

Herb-Marinated Grilled Portobello Mushrooms

Ingredients:

- 4 large portobello mushrooms, stems removed
- 1/4 cup balsamic vinegar
- 2 tablespoons soy sauce
- 2 tablespoons olive oil
- 2 cloves garlic, minced
- 1 teaspoon Dijon mustard
- 1 teaspoon dried thyme
- 1 teaspoon dried rosemary
- Salt and black pepper, to taste
- Fresh parsley, chopped, for garnish (optional)

Instructions:

1. Prepare Marinade:

- In a bowl, whisk together balsamic vinegar, soy sauce, olive oil, minced garlic, Dijon mustard, dried thyme, dried rosemary, salt, and black pepper.

2. Marinate Portobello Mushrooms:

- Place the cleaned portobello mushrooms in a shallow dish or a resealable plastic bag.
- Pour the marinade over the mushrooms, ensuring they are well-coated.
- Allow the mushrooms to marinate for at least 30 minutes, or longer for enhanced flavor. You can refrigerate them during marination.

3. Preheat Grill:

- Preheat your grill to medium-high heat.

4. Grill Portobello Mushrooms:

- Remove the mushrooms from the marinade and place them on the preheated grill.
- Grill for 4-6 minutes per side or until the mushrooms are tender and have nice grill marks.

5. Baste with Marinade (Optional):

- If desired, baste the mushrooms with the remaining marinade during grilling for extra flavor.

6. Garnish and Serve:

- Sprinkle the grilled portobello mushrooms with fresh chopped parsley if desired.
- Serve the mushrooms on a platter as a main course or a side dish.

7. Optional Serving Suggestions:

- Serve the grilled portobello mushrooms on a bun with your favorite burger toppings for a delicious vegetarian burger.
- Slice them and add to salads, sandwiches, or pasta dishes.

These Herb-Marinated Grilled Portobello Mushrooms are a fantastic option for a meatless meal with rich, savory flavors. Enjoy the versatility of this dish in various culinary applications!

Spinach and Artichoke Stuffed Chicken Breast

Ingredients:

For the Spinach and Artichoke Filling:

- 1 cup fresh spinach, chopped
- 1/2 cup artichoke hearts, chopped (canned or frozen and thawed)
- 1/2 cup cream cheese, softened
- 1/4 cup grated Parmesan cheese
- 1/4 cup shredded mozzarella cheese
- 2 cloves garlic, minced
- Salt and black pepper, to taste

For the Chicken:

- 4 boneless, skinless chicken breasts
- Salt and black pepper, to taste
- 1 tablespoon olive oil
- Paprika, for sprinkling
- Fresh parsley, chopped, for garnish (optional)

Instructions:

1. Prepare Spinach and Artichoke Filling:

- In a bowl, combine chopped spinach, chopped artichoke hearts, softened cream cheese, grated Parmesan cheese, shredded mozzarella cheese, minced garlic, salt, and black pepper. Mix well to create the filling.

2. Butterfly Chicken Breasts:

- Preheat the oven to 375°F (190°C).
- Lay each chicken breast flat on a cutting board. Use a sharp knife to cut a horizontal slit along the side of each breast, creating a pocket without cutting all the way through.

3. Stuff Chicken Breasts:

- Stuff each chicken breast with a generous amount of the spinach and artichoke filling, pressing it down to distribute evenly.

4. Season Chicken:

- Season the stuffed chicken breasts with salt and black pepper.
- Drizzle olive oil over the chicken breasts and sprinkle with paprika for color.

5. Sear Chicken:

- In an oven-safe skillet, heat olive oil over medium-high heat.
- Sear the stuffed chicken breasts for 2-3 minutes per side, or until golden brown.

6. Bake:

- Transfer the skillet to the preheated oven and bake for 20-25 minutes or until the chicken is cooked through and reaches an internal temperature of 165°F (74°C).

7. Garnish and Serve:

- Remove the stuffed chicken breasts from the oven.
- Garnish with fresh chopped parsley if desired.
- Serve the Spinach and Artichoke Stuffed Chicken Breast hot, either as is or with a side of your favorite vegetables or salad.

This Spinach and Artichoke Stuffed Chicken Breast is a delightful combination of creamy, cheesy filling and juicy chicken. It's perfect for a special dinner or whenever you want to impress with a delicious and elegant dish. Enjoy!

Lemon Garlic Shrimp Pasta with Cherry Tomatoes

Ingredients:

- 8 oz (about 225g) linguine or your favorite pasta
- 1 pound large shrimp, peeled and deveined
- Salt and black pepper, to taste
- 3 tablespoons olive oil
- 4 cloves garlic, minced
- 1 pint cherry tomatoes, halved
- Zest of 1 lemon
- Juice of 1 lemon
- Red pepper flakes, to taste (optional)
- Fresh parsley, chopped, for garnish
- Grated Parmesan cheese, for serving (optional)

Instructions:

1. Cook Pasta:

- Cook the pasta according to the package instructions in a large pot of salted boiling water. Drain and set aside.

2. Season and Cook Shrimp:

- Season the shrimp with salt and black pepper.
- In a large skillet, heat 2 tablespoons of olive oil over medium-high heat.
- Add the shrimp to the skillet and cook for 1-2 minutes per side or until they turn pink and opaque.
- Remove the shrimp from the skillet and set aside.

3. Sauté Garlic and Tomatoes:

- In the same skillet, add the remaining 1 tablespoon of olive oil.
- Add minced garlic and sauté for about 30 seconds until fragrant.
- Add halved cherry tomatoes to the skillet and cook for 2-3 minutes until they start to soften.

4. Combine Shrimp and Pasta:

- Return the cooked shrimp to the skillet with the tomatoes and garlic.

5. Add Lemon Zest and Juice:

- Add lemon zest and lemon juice to the skillet, stirring to combine.
- Optional: Add red pepper flakes for a bit of heat.

6. Toss with Pasta:

- Add the cooked pasta to the skillet with the shrimp, tomatoes, and garlic.
- Toss everything together until well coated with the lemon-garlic sauce.

7. Garnish and Serve:

- Garnish the Lemon Garlic Shrimp Pasta with Cherry Tomatoes with chopped fresh parsley.
- Serve hot, and optionally, sprinkle with grated Parmesan cheese.

Enjoy your Lemon Garlic Shrimp Pasta with Cherry Tomatoes, a delightful dish that's quick to prepare and bursting with bright and savory flavors!

Avocado Lime Cilantro Rice Bowl

Ingredients:

For the Rice Bowl:

- 1 cup cooked rice (white or brown)
- 1 ripe avocado, sliced
- 1 cup black beans, drained and rinsed
- 1 cup corn kernels (fresh, frozen, or canned)
- Cherry tomatoes, halved
- Red onion, finely chopped
- Fresh cilantro, chopped
- Lime wedges, for serving

For the Avocado Lime Cilantro Dressing:

- 1 ripe avocado
- 1/4 cup fresh cilantro, chopped
- Juice of 2 limes
- 2 tablespoons olive oil
- Salt and black pepper, to taste

Instructions:

1. Prepare the Rice Bowl:

- In each serving bowl, arrange a portion of cooked rice, sliced avocado, black beans, corn kernels, cherry tomatoes, and chopped red onion.

2. Make the Avocado Lime Cilantro Dressing:

- In a blender or food processor, combine a ripe avocado, chopped cilantro, lime juice, olive oil, salt, and black pepper.
- Blend until smooth and creamy.

3. Assemble the Bowl:

- Drizzle the Avocado Lime Cilantro Dressing over the rice bowl.

4. Garnish:

- Sprinkle fresh cilantro on top for an extra burst of flavor.

5. Serve:

- Serve the Avocado Lime Cilantro Rice Bowl with lime wedges on the side.

Enjoy this refreshing and nutritious Avocado Lime Cilantro Rice Bowl as a light and satisfying meal. The combination of creamy avocado, zesty lime, and aromatic cilantro creates a delicious and vibrant dish.

Pan-Seared Gnocchi with Brown Butter and Sage

Ingredients:

- 1 pound store-bought or homemade gnocchi
- 4 tablespoons unsalted butter
- Fresh sage leaves
- Salt and black pepper, to taste
- Grated Parmesan cheese, for serving

Instructions:

1. Cook Gnocchi:

- Cook the gnocchi according to the package instructions or until they float to the surface of boiling water. If using homemade gnocchi, they usually cook faster, so keep an eye on them.

2. Brown Butter:

- In a large skillet, melt the butter over medium heat. Continue cooking, swirling the pan occasionally, until the butter turns a golden brown color. Be careful not to burn it.

3. Add Sage:

- Add fresh sage leaves to the brown butter. Allow them to sizzle and become crispy, infusing the butter with their flavor.

4. Pan-Seared Gnocchi:

- Drain the cooked gnocchi and add them directly to the skillet with the brown butter and sage.
- Toss the gnocchi gently to coat them in the brown butter and allow them to develop a golden sear.

5. Season:

- Season the pan-seared gnocchi with salt and black pepper to taste. Adjust the seasoning as needed.

6. Serve:

- Transfer the pan-seared gnocchi to serving plates.
- Garnish with additional fresh sage leaves and grated Parmesan cheese.

7. Optional: Add Nutty Flavors:

- If desired, you can enhance the dish with a squeeze of lemon juice or a sprinkle of toasted pine nuts for added flavor.

8. Enjoy:

- Serve the Pan-Seared Gnocchi with Brown Butter and Sage immediately while the gnocchi are hot and the sage is crispy.

This simple yet flavorful dish is perfect for a quick and satisfying meal. The combination of pan-seared gnocchi, nutty brown butter, and aromatic sage creates a comforting and indulgent experience. Enjoy!

Harissa Grilled Eggplant with Yogurt Sauce

Ingredients:

For the Harissa Grilled Eggplant:

- 2 large eggplants, sliced into 1/2-inch rounds
- 2 tablespoons harissa paste
- 3 tablespoons olive oil
- Salt and black pepper, to taste
- Fresh parsley, chopped, for garnish

For the Yogurt Sauce:

- 1 cup Greek yogurt
- 1 clove garlic, minced
- 1 tablespoon lemon juice
- 1 tablespoon fresh mint, chopped
- Salt and black pepper, to taste

Instructions:

1. Prepare Harissa Marinade:

- In a bowl, whisk together harissa paste, olive oil, salt, and black pepper to create the marinade.

2. Marinate Eggplant:

- Brush both sides of the eggplant slices with the harissa marinade, ensuring they are well-coated. Allow them to marinate for at least 30 minutes.

3. Preheat Grill:

- Preheat your grill or grill pan over medium-high heat.

4. Grill Eggplant:

- Grill the marinated eggplant slices for 3-4 minutes per side or until they are tender and have grill marks.

5. Make Yogurt Sauce:

- In a small bowl, combine Greek yogurt, minced garlic, lemon juice, chopped fresh mint, salt, and black pepper. Mix well to create the yogurt sauce.

6. Serve:

- Arrange the Harissa Grilled Eggplant on a serving platter.
- Drizzle the yogurt sauce over the grilled eggplant.
- Garnish with chopped fresh parsley.

7. Optional: Add a Drizzle of Olive Oil:

- For an extra touch of richness, you can drizzle a bit of olive oil over the dish before serving.

8. Enjoy:

- Serve the Harissa Grilled Eggplant with Yogurt Sauce as a flavorful and satisfying appetizer or side dish.

This dish combines bold and spicy flavors with the creaminess of yogurt, creating a delicious harmony. The grilled eggplant absorbs the smoky harissa marinade, and the yogurt sauce adds a refreshing and cooling element. Enjoy the delightful contrasts in this Harissa Grilled Eggplant with Yogurt Sauce!

Cucumber Dill Greek Yogurt Dip with Pita Chips

Ingredients:

For the Cucumber Dill Greek Yogurt Dip:

- 1 cup Greek yogurt
- 1/2 cucumber, finely diced
- 1-2 tablespoons fresh dill, chopped
- 1 clove garlic, minced
- 1 tablespoon extra-virgin olive oil
- 1 teaspoon lemon juice
- Salt and black pepper, to taste

For the Pita Chips:

- Pita bread
- Olive oil
- Salt
- Paprika (optional)

Instructions:

1. Prepare Cucumber Dill Greek Yogurt Dip:

- In a bowl, combine Greek yogurt, finely diced cucumber, chopped fresh dill, minced garlic, extra-virgin olive oil, lemon juice, salt, and black pepper.
- Mix well until all the ingredients are evenly incorporated.
- Taste and adjust the seasonings as needed.

2. Make Pita Chips:

- Preheat your oven to 375°F (190°C).
- Cut pita bread into triangles or desired shapes.
- Place the pita triangles on a baking sheet.
- Brush the pita triangles lightly with olive oil.
- Sprinkle with salt and, if desired, paprika for added flavor.

- Bake in the preheated oven for 8-10 minutes or until the pita chips are golden and crispy.

3. Serve:

- Allow the pita chips to cool slightly before serving.
- Serve the Cucumber Dill Greek Yogurt Dip with the homemade pita chips.

4. Optional Garnish:

- Garnish the dip with additional fresh dill or a drizzle of olive oil, if desired.

This Cucumber Dill Greek Yogurt Dip with Pita Chips is not only delicious but also a healthier alternative to traditional dips. It's perfect for parties, gatherings, or simply as a wholesome snack. Enjoy!

Hoisin Glazed Tofu Stir-Fry

Ingredients:

For the Hoisin Glazed Tofu:

- 1 block extra-firm tofu, pressed and cubed
- 2 tablespoons hoisin sauce
- 1 tablespoon soy sauce
- 1 tablespoon rice vinegar
- 1 tablespoon sesame oil
- 1 tablespoon cornstarch
- 2 tablespoons vegetable oil (for cooking)

For the Stir-Fry:

- 1 tablespoon vegetable oil
- 1 bell pepper, sliced
- 1 carrot, julienned
- 1 broccoli crown, cut into florets
- 2 cups snap peas, trimmed
- 3 green onions, sliced (for garnish)
- Sesame seeds (for garnish, optional)
- Cooked rice or noodles (for serving)

Instructions:

1. Prepare the Hoisin Glazed Tofu:

- In a bowl, whisk together hoisin sauce, soy sauce, rice vinegar, sesame oil, and cornstarch to create the glaze.
- Add the cubed tofu to the glaze, ensuring each piece is well-coated. Allow it to marinate for at least 15-30 minutes.
- Heat 2 tablespoons of vegetable oil in a pan over medium-high heat.
- Add the marinated tofu and cook until all sides are golden and crispy. Set aside.

2. Stir-Fry Vegetables:

- In the same pan, add 1 tablespoon of vegetable oil.
- Add sliced bell pepper, julienned carrot, broccoli florets, and snap peas. Stir-fry for 3-5 minutes until the vegetables are tender-crisp.

3. Combine Tofu and Vegetables:

- Add the cooked hoisin glazed tofu back to the pan with the stir-fried vegetables. Toss everything together to combine.

4. Serve:

- Serve the Hoisin Glazed Tofu Stir-Fry over cooked rice or noodles.

5. Garnish:

- Garnish with sliced green onions and sesame seeds for extra flavor and texture.

Enjoy this Hoisin Glazed Tofu Stir-Fry as a delicious and satisfying vegetarian meal. The hoisin sauce adds a rich and savory sweetness that complements the tofu and colorful vegetables perfectly.

Mango Avocado Salsa with Grilled Chicken

Ingredients:

For the Grilled Chicken:

- 4 boneless, skinless chicken breasts
- 2 tablespoons olive oil
- 1 teaspoon ground cumin
- 1 teaspoon smoked paprika
- Salt and black pepper, to taste
- Lime wedges, for serving

For the Mango Avocado Salsa:

- 2 ripe mangos, diced
- 2 ripe avocados, diced
- 1/2 red onion, finely chopped
- 1/4 cup fresh cilantro, chopped
- 1 jalapeño, seeds removed and finely chopped (optional for heat)
- Juice of 2 limes
- Salt and black pepper, to taste

Instructions:

1. Prepare Grilled Chicken:

- Preheat the grill to medium-high heat.
- In a bowl, mix olive oil, ground cumin, smoked paprika, salt, and black pepper.
- Brush the chicken breasts with the spice mixture.
- Grill the chicken for about 6-8 minutes per side or until fully cooked with grill marks.
- Once done, let the chicken rest for a few minutes before slicing.

2. Make Mango Avocado Salsa:

- In a separate bowl, combine diced mangos, diced avocados, finely chopped red onion, chopped cilantro, and jalapeño (if using).
- Squeeze lime juice over the salsa and gently toss to combine.
- Season with salt and black pepper to taste.

3. Assemble:

- Arrange the sliced grilled chicken on a serving platter.
- Top the chicken with generous servings of the Mango Avocado Salsa.

4. Serve:

- Serve the Mango Avocado Salsa with Grilled Chicken with additional lime wedges on the side.

This dish is not only visually appealing but also bursting with flavors. The sweetness of mango and creaminess of avocado perfectly complement the smoky grilled chicken. It's a delightful and healthy meal, perfect for a light lunch or dinner. Enjoy!

Smoked Salmon and Cream Cheese Cucumber Bites

Ingredients:

- English cucumbers, sliced into rounds
- Smoked salmon slices
- Cream cheese, softened
- Fresh dill, chopped
- Capers (optional, for garnish)
- Lemon wedges (for serving)
- Black pepper, to taste

Instructions:

1. Prepare Cucumber Slices:

- Wash the English cucumbers and slice them into rounds, each about 1/2 inch thick.

2. Assemble Cucumber Bites:

- Place the cucumber rounds on a serving platter.
- Spread a small amount of softened cream cheese on each cucumber slice.
- Top the cream cheese with a piece of smoked salmon.

3. Garnish:

- Sprinkle chopped fresh dill over the smoked salmon.
- Optionally, add a few capers on top of each bite for extra flavor.

4. Serve:

- Arrange the Smoked Salmon and Cream Cheese Cucumber Bites on a serving platter.
- Squeeze a bit of fresh lemon juice over the bites just before serving.
- Optionally, add a pinch of black pepper for extra seasoning.

5. Enjoy:

- Serve immediately and enjoy these delicious and visually appealing appetizers!

These bites are not only easy to assemble but also offer a perfect balance of textures and flavors. They make for a fantastic addition to any party or gathering. Enjoy!

Quick and Easy Beef and Broccoli

Ingredients:

- 1 lb (450g) flank steak, thinly sliced against the grain
- 3 cups broccoli florets
- 3 tablespoons soy sauce
- 2 tablespoons oyster sauce
- 1 tablespoon hoisin sauce
- 1 tablespoon cornstarch
- 2 tablespoons vegetable oil, divided
- 3 cloves garlic, minced
- 1 tablespoon fresh ginger, grated
- 1/4 cup water
- Sesame seeds and sliced green onions for garnish (optional)
- Cooked rice for serving

Instructions:

1. Prepare the Beef:

- In a bowl, mix the thinly sliced flank steak with soy sauce, oyster sauce, hoisin sauce, and cornstarch. Allow it to marinate for about 15-30 minutes.

2. Cook the Broccoli:

- In a large pan or wok, heat 1 tablespoon of vegetable oil over medium-high heat.
- Add the broccoli florets and stir-fry for 2-3 minutes until they are tender-crisp. Remove the broccoli from the pan and set aside.

3. Cook the Beef:

- In the same pan, add another tablespoon of vegetable oil.
- Add the marinated beef slices and stir-fry for 2-3 minutes until they are browned and cooked through.
- Add the minced garlic and grated ginger, and stir-fry for an additional 1-2 minutes until fragrant.

4. Combine and Sauce:

- Return the cooked broccoli to the pan with the beef.
- Add water and stir to combine everything.

5. Finish and Serve:

- Cook for an additional 1-2 minutes until the sauce thickens slightly and coats the beef and broccoli.
- Garnish with sesame seeds and sliced green onions if desired.

6. Serve:

- Serve the quick and easy Beef and Broccoli over cooked rice.

This dish comes together in no time and is full of savory flavors. Adjust the sauce ingredients to your taste preference, and feel free to add a pinch of red pepper flakes for a bit of heat. Enjoy your delicious and speedy Beef and Broccoli stir-fry!

Lemon Thyme Grilled Swordfish

Ingredients:

- 4 swordfish steaks (about 6 ounces each)
- 2 tablespoons olive oil
- Zest and juice of 1 lemon
- 2 tablespoons fresh thyme leaves, chopped
- 3 cloves garlic, minced
- Salt and black pepper, to taste
- Lemon wedges, for serving

Instructions:

1. Prepare the Marinade:

- In a bowl, combine olive oil, lemon zest, lemon juice, chopped thyme, minced garlic, salt, and black pepper.

2. Marinate the Swordfish:

- Place the swordfish steaks in a shallow dish or a resealable plastic bag.
- Pour the marinade over the swordfish, ensuring each steak is well-coated. Allow it to marinate for at least 30 minutes, or refrigerate for up to 2 hours.

3. Preheat the Grill:

- Preheat your grill to medium-high heat.

4. Grill the Swordfish:

- Remove the swordfish from the marinade and discard the marinade.
- Grill the swordfish steaks for about 4-5 minutes per side, or until they are cooked through and have nice grill marks. The internal temperature should reach 145°F (63°C).

5. Serve:

- Remove the swordfish from the grill and let it rest for a few minutes.
- Serve the Lemon Thyme Grilled Swordfish with lemon wedges on the side.

6. Optional Garnish:

- Garnish with additional fresh thyme leaves for a burst of color and flavor.

Enjoy the light and citrusy taste of Lemon Thyme Grilled Swordfish, a perfect dish for a summer barbecue or a quick and delicious weeknight meal. Serve it with your favorite sides like a fresh salad or grilled vegetables.

Quinoa Salad with Roasted Vegetables and Feta

Ingredients:

For the Quinoa Salad:

- 1 cup quinoa, rinsed
- 2 cups water or vegetable broth
- 1 red bell pepper, diced
- 1 yellow bell pepper, diced
- 1 zucchini, diced
- 1 red onion, diced
- 1 cup cherry tomatoes, halved
- 3 tablespoons olive oil
- Salt and black pepper, to taste
- 1/4 cup fresh parsley, chopped
- 1/4 cup fresh basil, chopped

For the Dressing:

- 3 tablespoons extra-virgin olive oil
- 2 tablespoons balsamic vinegar
- 1 clove garlic, minced
- Salt and black pepper, to taste

For the Toppings:

- 1/2 cup crumbled feta cheese
- Optional: Toasted pine nuts or chopped walnuts

Instructions:

1. Roast the Vegetables:

- Preheat the oven to 400°F (200°C).
- In a large bowl, toss the diced red and yellow bell peppers, zucchini, red onion, and cherry tomatoes with olive oil, salt, and black pepper.

- Spread the vegetables on a baking sheet in a single layer.
- Roast in the preheated oven for 20-25 minutes or until the vegetables are tender and slightly caramelized.

2. Cook the Quinoa:

- In a saucepan, combine quinoa and water or vegetable broth. Bring to a boil, then reduce heat to low, cover, and simmer for 15-20 minutes or until the quinoa is cooked and water is absorbed.
- Fluff the quinoa with a fork and let it cool slightly.

3. Prepare the Dressing:

- In a small bowl, whisk together olive oil, balsamic vinegar, minced garlic, salt, and black pepper.

4. Assemble the Salad:

- In a large serving bowl, combine the cooked quinoa and roasted vegetables.
- Add the chopped fresh parsley and basil.
- Drizzle the dressing over the salad and toss gently to combine.

5. Garnish:

- Top the quinoa salad with crumbled feta cheese and, if desired, toasted pine nuts or chopped walnuts.

6. Serve:

- Serve the Quinoa Salad with Roasted Vegetables and Feta at room temperature or chilled.

This Quinoa Salad is not only nutritious but also bursting with colors and flavors. It makes for a satisfying and versatile meal on its own or as a side dish. Enjoy!

Spicy Garlic Butter Shrimp Tacos

Ingredients:

For the Spicy Garlic Butter Shrimp:

- 1 pound large shrimp, peeled and deveined
- 4 tablespoons unsalted butter
- 4 cloves garlic, minced
- 1 teaspoon smoked paprika
- 1/2 teaspoon cayenne pepper (adjust to taste for spiciness)
- Salt and black pepper, to taste
- Juice of 1 lime
- Fresh cilantro, chopped, for garnish

For the Taco Assembly:

- Flour or corn tortillas
- Shredded cabbage or lettuce
- Sliced avocado
- Salsa or pico de gallo
- Lime wedges

Instructions:

1. Prepare the Spicy Garlic Butter Shrimp:

- In a large skillet over medium-high heat, melt the butter.
- Add minced garlic and cook for 1-2 minutes until fragrant.
- Add the shrimp to the skillet and cook for 2-3 minutes per side or until they are pink and opaque.
- Sprinkle smoked paprika, cayenne pepper, salt, and black pepper over the shrimp. Toss to coat evenly.
- Squeeze lime juice over the shrimp and toss again.
- Garnish with chopped fresh cilantro and remove from heat.

2. Warm the Tortillas:

- Heat the tortillas in a dry skillet or microwave until warm and pliable.

3. Assemble the Tacos:

- Place a spoonful of the Spicy Garlic Butter Shrimp onto each tortilla.
- Top with shredded cabbage or lettuce, sliced avocado, and your choice of salsa or pico de gallo.

4. Serve:

- Serve the Spicy Garlic Butter Shrimp Tacos with lime wedges on the side.

Enjoy these delicious and spicy shrimp tacos as a flavorful and quick meal. The combination of garlic, butter, and spices adds a delightful kick to the succulent shrimp, creating a satisfying taco experience.

Caprese Stuffed Portobello Mushrooms

Ingredients:

- 4 large portobello mushrooms, stems removed
- 1 cup cherry tomatoes, halved
- 1 cup fresh mozzarella, diced
- 1/4 cup fresh basil, chopped
- 2 tablespoons balsamic glaze
- 2 tablespoons olive oil
- Salt and black pepper, to taste

Instructions:

1. Prepare the Portobello Mushrooms:

- Preheat the oven to 400°F (200°C).
- Clean the portobello mushrooms and remove the stems.
- Brush the mushroom caps with olive oil on both sides and place them on a baking sheet.

2. Prepare the Filling:

- In a bowl, combine cherry tomatoes, fresh mozzarella, and chopped fresh basil.

3. Stuff the Mushrooms:

- Spoon the tomato, mozzarella, and basil mixture into the cavity of each portobello mushroom.

4. Bake:

- Bake the stuffed portobello mushrooms in the preheated oven for 15-20 minutes, or until the mushrooms are tender and the cheese is melted and bubbly.

5. Finish and Serve:

- Remove the mushrooms from the oven and drizzle balsamic glaze over each stuffed mushroom.
- Season with salt and black pepper to taste.
- Serve the Caprese Stuffed Portobello Mushrooms warm.

Enjoy these Caprese Stuffed Portobello Mushrooms as a delightful appetizer or a light main dish. The combination of juicy tomatoes, creamy mozzarella, and fragrant basil nestled in the earthy portobello mushrooms creates a burst of flavor in every bite.

Baked Brie with Honey and Walnuts

Ingredients:

- 1 wheel of Brie cheese (about 8-12 ounces)
- 1/4 cup chopped walnuts
- 2 tablespoons honey
- Fresh rosemary sprigs (optional, for garnish)
- Crackers or sliced baguette, for serving

Instructions:

1. Preheat the Oven:

- Preheat your oven to 350°F (175°C).

2. Prepare the Brie:

- Place the Brie wheel on a baking dish or a small oven-safe skillet.
- Optionally, you can score the top of the Brie with a knife to allow the honey to seep into the cheese.

3. Add Walnuts:

- Sprinkle the chopped walnuts evenly over the top of the Brie.

4. Drizzle with Honey:

- Drizzle the honey over the Brie and walnuts, ensuring it's evenly distributed.

5. Bake:

- Bake in the preheated oven for 12-15 minutes or until the Brie is soft and gooey, and the nuts are toasted.

6. Garnish:

- If desired, garnish with fresh rosemary sprigs for a pop of color and aroma.

7. Serve:

- Transfer the baked Brie to a serving platter.
- Serve it immediately with crackers or sliced baguette for dipping.

Enjoy this Baked Brie with Honey and Walnuts as a warm and gooey appetizer that's perfect for sharing. The combination of melted Brie, sweet honey, and crunchy walnuts creates a flavor profile that is both comforting and sophisticated.

Mediterranean Tuna Salad Wraps

Ingredients:

For the Tuna Salad:

- 2 cans (5 ounces each) canned tuna, drained
- 1/2 cup cherry tomatoes, halved
- 1/4 cup Kalamata olives, sliced
- 1/4 cup red onion, finely chopped
- 1/4 cup cucumber, diced
- 2 tablespoons feta cheese, crumbled
- 2 tablespoons fresh parsley, chopped
- 2 tablespoons extra-virgin olive oil
- 1 tablespoon lemon juice
- Salt and black pepper, to taste

For the Wraps:

- Whole-grain or spinach wraps or tortillas
- Fresh spinach or mixed greens

Instructions:

1. Prepare the Tuna Salad:

- In a large bowl, combine drained tuna, cherry tomatoes, Kalamata olives, red onion, cucumber, feta cheese, and fresh parsley.
- In a small bowl, whisk together extra-virgin olive oil, lemon juice, salt, and black pepper.
- Pour the dressing over the tuna mixture and toss until everything is well coated.

2. Assemble the Wraps:

- Lay out the wraps on a clean surface.
- Place a handful of fresh spinach or mixed greens in the center of each wrap.
- Spoon the Mediterranean tuna salad mixture over the greens.

3. Wrap and Serve:

- Fold in the sides of the wrap and then roll it up tightly from the bottom.
- Repeat with the remaining wraps.
- Slice the wraps in half diagonally if desired.

4. Serve:

- Serve the Mediterranean Tuna Salad Wraps immediately.

These wraps are not only delicious but also packed with Mediterranean flavors. The combination of tuna, olives, feta, and fresh veggies creates a light and satisfying meal. Enjoy these wraps for a quick and healthy lunch or dinner option.

Pistachio-Crusted Dijon Salmon

Ingredients:

- 4 salmon fillets
- 1 cup unsalted pistachios, shelled
- 2 tablespoons Dijon mustard
- 2 tablespoons honey
- 2 tablespoons olive oil
- 1 tablespoon lemon juice
- Salt and black pepper, to taste
- Fresh parsley, chopped, for garnish (optional)

Instructions:

1. Preheat the Oven:

- Preheat your oven to 400°F (200°C).

2. Prepare the Pistachio Crust:

- In a food processor, pulse the pistachios until finely chopped. Be careful not to over-process; you want a coarse texture.

3. Prepare the Dijon Glaze:

- In a small bowl, whisk together Dijon mustard, honey, olive oil, lemon juice, salt, and black pepper.

4. Coat the Salmon:

- Place the salmon fillets on a parchment paper-lined baking sheet.
- Brush each salmon fillet with the Dijon glaze.
- Press the chopped pistachios onto the top of each salmon fillet, coating them evenly.

5. Bake:

- Bake in the preheated oven for 12-15 minutes or until the salmon is cooked through and the pistachio crust is golden and crispy.

6. Garnish and Serve:

    - Remove the salmon from the oven and garnish with chopped fresh parsley if desired.
    - Serve the Pistachio-Crusted Dijon Salmon with your favorite side dishes.

This dish offers a perfect balance of textures and flavors, with the nutty crunch of pistachios complementing the tender and flaky salmon. The Dijon mustard glaze adds a zesty kick to the overall taste. Enjoy this Pistachio-Crusted Dijon Salmon for a delicious and elegant meal.

Pomegranate and Goat Cheese Spinach Salad

Ingredients:

For the Salad:

- 6 cups fresh baby spinach leaves, washed and dried
- 1 cup pomegranate seeds
- 1/2 cup crumbled goat cheese
- 1/4 cup chopped pecans or walnuts (optional)
- 1/4 cup red onion, thinly sliced

For the Dressing:

- 3 tablespoons extra-virgin olive oil
- 1 tablespoon balsamic vinegar
- 1 teaspoon Dijon mustard
- 1 teaspoon honey
- Salt and black pepper, to taste

Instructions:

1. Prepare the Salad:

- In a large salad bowl, combine the fresh baby spinach, pomegranate seeds, crumbled goat cheese, chopped nuts (if using), and thinly sliced red onion.

2. Make the Dressing:

- In a small bowl, whisk together the extra-virgin olive oil, balsamic vinegar, Dijon mustard, honey, salt, and black pepper.

3. Toss the Salad:

- Drizzle the dressing over the salad ingredients.
- Toss the salad gently to ensure the dressing is evenly distributed.

4. Serve:

- Serve the Pomegranate and Goat Cheese Spinach Salad immediately.

This salad is not only visually appealing but also a delightful combination of flavors and textures. The sweet bursts of pomegranate seeds, the creamy goat cheese, and the crisp spinach create a perfect balance. It's an excellent side salad for a variety of meals or a light and healthy main dish on its own. Enjoy!

Basil Pesto Pasta with Cherry Tomatoes

Ingredients:

- 8 ounces (about 225g) of your favorite pasta (such as spaghetti or penne)
- 1 cup fresh basil leaves, packed
- 1/2 cup grated Parmesan cheese
- 1/3 cup pine nuts
- 2 garlic cloves, peeled
- 1/2 cup extra-virgin olive oil
- Salt and black pepper, to taste
- 1 cup cherry tomatoes, halved
- Grated Parmesan for serving (optional)
- Fresh basil leaves for garnish (optional)

Instructions:

1. Cook the Pasta:

- Cook the pasta according to the package instructions until al dente. Drain and set aside.

2. Make the Basil Pesto:

- In a food processor, combine fresh basil, grated Parmesan cheese, pine nuts, and peeled garlic cloves.
- Pulse the ingredients until finely chopped.
- With the food processor running, slowly stream in the olive oil until the pesto reaches a smooth consistency.
- Season with salt and black pepper to taste. Adjust the seasoning if needed.

3. Toss with Pasta:

- In a large mixing bowl, combine the cooked pasta with the basil pesto. Toss until the pasta is well coated with the pesto.

4. Add Cherry Tomatoes:

- Gently fold in the halved cherry tomatoes, distributing them evenly throughout the pasta.

5. Serve:

- Serve the Basil Pesto Pasta with Cherry Tomatoes.
- Optionally, garnish with additional grated Parmesan and fresh basil leaves.

This dish is a celebration of fresh flavors, and the combination of basil pesto and sweet cherry tomatoes is a classic and delightful pairing. It's a quick and satisfying meal that can be enjoyed on its own or as a side dish. Enjoy your Basil Pesto Pasta with Cherry Tomatoes!

Lemon Rosemary Grilled Chicken Skewers

Ingredients:

- 1.5 lbs (about 680g) boneless, skinless chicken breasts, cut into bite-sized cubes
- Zest and juice of 1 lemon
- 2 tablespoons fresh rosemary, finely chopped
- 3 cloves garlic, minced
- 1/4 cup extra-virgin olive oil
- Salt and black pepper, to taste
- Wooden or metal skewers

Instructions:

1. Marinate the Chicken:

- In a bowl, combine the lemon zest, lemon juice, chopped rosemary, minced garlic, olive oil, salt, and black pepper.
- Add the chicken cubes to the marinade, making sure they are well-coated. Allow the chicken to marinate for at least 30 minutes, or refrigerate for up to 4 hours for more flavor.

2. Preheat the Grill:

- Preheat your grill to medium-high heat.

3. Skewer the Chicken:

- If using wooden skewers, soak them in water for about 30 minutes to prevent burning.
- Thread the marinated chicken cubes onto the skewers.

4. Grill the Chicken:

- Place the chicken skewers on the preheated grill.
- Grill for about 8-10 minutes, turning occasionally, or until the chicken is cooked through and has a nice char on the outside.

5. Serve:

- Remove the Lemon Rosemary Grilled Chicken Skewers from the grill.
- Serve the skewers hot with your favorite side dishes.

6. Optional Garnish:

- Garnish with additional fresh rosemary and lemon wedges for extra flavor.

These Lemon Rosemary Grilled Chicken Skewers are not only easy to make but also bursting with citrusy and herby goodness. They are perfect for a summer barbecue or a quick and delicious weeknight meal. Enjoy!

Shrimp and Avocado Ceviche

Ingredients:

- 1 pound large shrimp, peeled, deveined, and chopped
- 1 cup cherry tomatoes, diced
- 1/2 red onion, finely chopped
- 1 cucumber, peeled and diced
- 2 avocados, diced
- 1 jalapeño, seeded and finely chopped (optional, for heat)
- 1/2 cup fresh cilantro, chopped
- Juice of 4-5 limes
- Salt and black pepper, to taste
- Tortilla chips or tostadas, for serving

Instructions:

1. Prepare the Shrimp:

- Bring a pot of salted water to a boil. Add the chopped shrimp and cook for about 2-3 minutes or until they turn pink and opaque.
- Drain the shrimp and place them in a large bowl.

2. Marinate the Shrimp:

- Add the diced cherry tomatoes, chopped red onion, diced cucumber, diced avocados, chopped jalapeño (if using), and chopped cilantro to the bowl with the shrimp.
- Squeeze the juice of 4-5 limes over the mixture.
- Season with salt and black pepper to taste.
- Gently toss the ingredients to combine.

3. Chill:

- Cover the bowl with plastic wrap and refrigerate the ceviche for at least 30 minutes to allow the flavors to meld.

4. Serve:

- Serve the Shrimp and Avocado Ceviche chilled.
- Optionally, garnish with additional cilantro and serve with tortilla chips or tostadas.

This Shrimp and Avocado Ceviche is perfect for a light and refreshing appetizer or a healthy snack. The combination of citrusy lime, succulent shrimp, creamy avocado, and fresh vegetables creates a delicious and satisfying dish. Enjoy!

Prosciutto-Wrapped Asparagus Bundles

Ingredients:

- 1 bunch of asparagus spears, woody ends trimmed
- Olive oil, for drizzling
- Salt and black pepper, to taste
- 8-10 slices of prosciutto

Instructions:

1. Preheat the Oven:

- Preheat your oven to 400°F (200°C).

2. Prepare the Asparagus:

- Drizzle the trimmed asparagus spears with olive oil and season with salt and black pepper. Toss to coat evenly.

3. Bundle the Asparagus:

- Take 4-5 asparagus spears and bundle them together.
- Wrap a slice of prosciutto around the center of each asparagus bundle, securing the spears together.
- Repeat for the remaining asparagus.

4. Arrange on a Baking Sheet:

- Place the prosciutto-wrapped asparagus bundles on a baking sheet lined with parchment paper.

5. Bake:

- Bake in the preheated oven for 12-15 minutes or until the asparagus is tender and the prosciutto is crispy.

6. Serve:

- Remove from the oven and transfer the prosciutto-wrapped asparagus bundles to a serving platter.
- Serve immediately.

These Prosciutto-Wrapped Asparagus Bundles make for a sophisticated appetizer or side dish. The combination of the salty prosciutto and the earthy asparagus creates a delightful flavor contrast. They are perfect for entertaining or as a special addition to your dinner table. Enjoy!

Sesame Ginger Quinoa Bowl with Vegetables

Ingredients:

For the Quinoa:

- 1 cup quinoa, rinsed
- 2 cups water
- 1/2 teaspoon salt

For the Vegetables:

- 2 cups broccoli florets
- 1 red bell pepper, thinly sliced
- 1 carrot, julienned
- 1 cup snap peas, trimmed
- 2 tablespoons sesame oil

For the Sesame Ginger Sauce:

- 3 tablespoons soy sauce
- 2 tablespoons rice vinegar
- 1 tablespoon sesame oil
- 1 tablespoon fresh ginger, grated
- 2 cloves garlic, minced
- 1 tablespoon honey or maple syrup (adjust to taste)
- 1 teaspoon sesame seeds (optional, for garnish)

Instructions:

Rinse the quinoa under cold water. In a medium saucepan, combine the quinoa, water, and salt. Bring to a boil, then reduce the heat to low, cover, and simmer for 15-20 minutes, or until the quinoa is cooked and water is absorbed. Fluff the quinoa with a fork and set aside.
In a large skillet or wok, heat 2 tablespoons of sesame oil over medium-high heat. Add the broccoli, red bell pepper, carrot, and snap peas. Stir-fry the vegetables for 5-7 minutes, or until they are tender-crisp.
In a small bowl, whisk together the soy sauce, rice vinegar, sesame oil, grated ginger, minced garlic, and honey (or maple syrup).

Pour the sesame ginger sauce over the stir-fried vegetables and toss to coat evenly. Cook for an additional 2 minutes, allowing the sauce to thicken slightly. Divide the cooked quinoa among serving bowls and top with the sesame ginger vegetables.
Garnish with sesame seeds, if desired.

Enjoy your delicious and nutritious Sesame Ginger Quinoa Bowl with Vegetables! Feel free to customize the recipe by adding your favorite protein such as tofu, chicken, or shrimp.

Grilled Halloumi and Watermelon Skewers

Ingredients:

- 250g halloumi cheese, cut into cubes
- 2 cups watermelon, cut into cubes
- 2 tablespoons olive oil
- 1 tablespoon fresh mint, finely chopped
- 1 tablespoon balsamic glaze (optional)
- Salt and pepper to taste
- Wooden skewers, soaked in water for 30 minutes

Instructions:

Preheat your grill or grill pan to medium-high heat.
In a bowl, toss the halloumi cubes with olive oil, fresh mint, salt, and pepper. Make sure the halloumi is well coated.
Assemble the skewers by alternating the halloumi cubes and watermelon cubes.
Place the skewers on the preheated grill. Grill for about 2-3 minutes per side, or until the halloumi develops a golden brown crust.
Remove the skewers from the grill and transfer them to a serving platter.
Drizzle the skewers with balsamic glaze if desired.
Serve immediately and enjoy these delicious Grilled Halloumi and Watermelon Skewers as a light and refreshing appetizer.

Feel free to get creative and add a squeeze of lime juice, a sprinkle of chili flakes, or any other herbs or spices to enhance the flavors. This dish is not only tasty but also visually appealing, making it a perfect addition to your summer gatherings.

Lemon Butter Cod with Garlic Parmesan Asparagus

Ingredients:

For the Lemon Butter Cod:

- 4 cod fillets
- Salt and black pepper to taste
- 2 tablespoons olive oil
- 4 tablespoons unsalted butter
- 3 cloves garlic, minced
- Zest of 1 lemon
- Juice of 1 lemon
- 2 tablespoons fresh parsley, chopped

For the Garlic Parmesan Asparagus:

- 1 bunch asparagus, trimmed
- 2 tablespoons olive oil
- 3 cloves garlic, minced
- 1/4 cup grated Parmesan cheese
- Salt and black pepper to taste

Instructions:

For the Lemon Butter Cod:

Preheat the oven to 400°F (200°C).
Season the cod fillets with salt and black pepper on both sides.
In a large oven-safe skillet, heat 2 tablespoons of olive oil over medium-high heat.
Add the cod fillets to the skillet and cook for 2-3 minutes per side, or until they develop a golden brown crust.
In the same skillet, add butter and minced garlic. Allow the butter to melt, and stir in lemon zest and lemon juice.
Spoon the lemon butter sauce over the cod fillets.
Transfer the skillet to the preheated oven and bake for about 10-12 minutes or until the cod is cooked through and flakes easily with a fork.
Sprinkle fresh parsley over the cod before serving.

For the Garlic Parmesan Asparagus:

While the cod is baking, prepare the asparagus. In a large bowl, toss the trimmed asparagus with olive oil, minced garlic, salt, and black pepper.
Spread the asparagus in a single layer on a baking sheet.
Roast the asparagus in the oven for about 8-10 minutes or until they are tender-crisp.
Remove the asparagus from the oven and sprinkle grated Parmesan cheese over the top.

Serve the Lemon Butter Cod over a bed of Garlic Parmesan Asparagus. This dish is not only delicious but also quick and easy to prepare. Enjoy your meal!

Balsamic Glazed Brussels Sprouts with Bacon

Ingredients:

- 1 lb Brussels sprouts, trimmed and halved
- 4 slices bacon, cooked and crumbled
- 2 tablespoons olive oil
- 2 tablespoons balsamic glaze
- Salt and black pepper to taste
- Optional: 1/4 cup grated Parmesan cheese for garnish
- Optional: Chopped fresh parsley for garnish

Instructions:

Preheat the oven to 400°F (200°C).
In a large bowl, toss the halved Brussels sprouts with olive oil, salt, and black pepper until they are evenly coated.
Spread the Brussels sprouts in a single layer on a baking sheet.
Roast the Brussels sprouts in the preheated oven for about 20-25 minutes or until they are golden brown and crisp on the edges, tossing halfway through for even cooking.
While the Brussels sprouts are roasting, cook the bacon slices until crispy. Once cooked, crumble the bacon into small pieces.
Remove the Brussels sprouts from the oven and drizzle the balsamic glaze over them. Toss to coat evenly.
Sprinkle the crumbled bacon over the Brussels sprouts.
Optional: Garnish with grated Parmesan cheese and chopped fresh parsley for added flavor.

Serve the Balsamic Glazed Brussels Sprouts with Bacon as a tasty side dish for your meal. The combination of the sweet and tangy balsamic glaze with the smoky bacon complements the roasted Brussels sprouts perfectly. Enjoy!

Tomato Basil Mozzarella Stacks

Ingredients:

- 4 large tomatoes, sliced
- 1 pound fresh mozzarella cheese, sliced
- Fresh basil leaves
- Extra virgin olive oil, for drizzling
- Balsamic glaze, for drizzling
- Salt and black pepper to taste

Instructions:

Slice the Tomatoes and Mozzarella:
- Wash and dry the tomatoes. Slice them into rounds, about 1/4-inch thick.
- Similarly, slice the fresh mozzarella into rounds, keeping them approximately the same thickness as the tomato slices.

Assemble the Stacks:
- Start assembling the stacks by layering a slice of tomato, followed by a slice of fresh mozzarella, and then a fresh basil leaf.
- Repeat the layering process until you have a stack of desired height. Aim to have three layers in each stack.

Drizzle with Olive Oil:
- Lightly drizzle extra virgin olive oil over the tomato, mozzarella, and basil stacks.

Season with Salt and Pepper:
- Sprinkle a pinch of salt and black pepper over each stack to enhance the flavors.

Drizzle with Balsamic Glaze:
- Finish the stacks by drizzling balsamic glaze over the top. This adds a sweet and tangy flavor to the dish.

Serve:
- Arrange the Tomato Basil Mozzarella Stacks on a serving platter or individual plates.

Optional Garnish:
- Optionally, you can garnish with additional fresh basil leaves and a sprinkle of extra salt and pepper.

These Tomato Basil Mozzarella Stacks make for a beautiful and delicious appetizer, showcasing the classic combination of flavors. They are perfect for summer gatherings or any occasion where you want a light and flavorful dish. Enjoy!

Quick and Easy Shrimp Scampi

Ingredients:

- 1 pound large shrimp, peeled and deveined
- 8 ounces linguine or spaghetti
- 3 tablespoons unsalted butter
- 3 tablespoons olive oil
- 4 cloves garlic, minced
- 1/2 teaspoon red pepper flakes (adjust to taste)
- 1/2 cup dry white wine
- Juice of 1 lemon
- Salt and black pepper to taste
- 1/4 cup fresh parsley, chopped
- Grated Parmesan cheese for serving (optional)

Instructions:

Prepare the Pasta:
- Cook the linguine or spaghetti according to the package instructions. Drain and set aside.

Cook the Shrimp:
- In a large skillet, heat 2 tablespoons of butter and 2 tablespoons of olive oil over medium-high heat.
- Add the minced garlic and red pepper flakes, sautéing for about 1 minute until the garlic is fragrant.

Add Shrimp:
- Add the shrimp to the skillet, spreading them in a single layer. Cook for 2-3 minutes or until they start to turn pink.

Deglaze with Wine:
- Pour in the white wine and lemon juice. Allow the mixture to simmer for another 2-3 minutes, or until the shrimp are fully cooked and opaque. Season with salt and black pepper to taste.

Finish the Dish:
- Stir in the remaining 1 tablespoon of butter and 1 tablespoon of olive oil.
- Add the cooked pasta to the skillet, tossing to coat it in the flavorful sauce.

Garnish and Serve:

- Sprinkle chopped fresh parsley over the shrimp and pasta. Toss once more to combine.
- Optionally, serve with grated Parmesan cheese on top.

Serve Immediately:
- Serve the Shrimp Scampi immediately while hot.

This quick and easy Shrimp Scampi is packed with flavor, and the combination of garlic, lemon, and wine creates a delicious sauce for the shrimp and pasta. Enjoy your meal!

Spinach and Feta Stuffed Chicken Breast

Ingredients:

- 4 boneless, skinless chicken breasts
- Salt and black pepper to taste
- 2 cups fresh spinach, chopped
- 1/2 cup feta cheese, crumbled
- 2 tablespoons olive oil
- 2 cloves garlic, minced
- 1 teaspoon dried oregano
- 1 teaspoon dried thyme
- 1 teaspoon paprika
- Toothpicks or kitchen twine

Instructions:

Preheat the Oven:
- Preheat your oven to 375°F (190°C).

Prepare the Spinach and Feta Filling:
- In a medium-sized bowl, combine the chopped spinach, crumbled feta cheese, minced garlic, oregano, thyme, and paprika. Mix well.

Butterfly the Chicken Breasts:
- Lay each chicken breast flat on a cutting board. Using a sharp knife, cut a pocket into each chicken breast by slicing horizontally, almost to the other side, but leaving the edges intact.

Season and Stuff the Chicken:
- Season the inside of each chicken breast with salt and black pepper.
- Stuff each chicken breast with the spinach and feta mixture, pressing it down gently.

Secure with Toothpicks or Kitchen Twine:
- If using toothpicks, secure the openings of the chicken breasts to keep the filling in place. Alternatively, you can tie them with kitchen twine.

Sear the Chicken:
- In an oven-safe skillet, heat olive oil over medium-high heat. Sear the stuffed chicken breasts for 2-3 minutes on each side, until golden brown.

Bake in the Oven:

- Transfer the skillet to the preheated oven and bake for about 20-25 minutes, or until the chicken is cooked through and reaches an internal temperature of 165°F (74°C).

Rest and Serve:
- Allow the stuffed chicken breasts to rest for a few minutes before slicing. This helps the juices redistribute.

Serve:
- Serve the Spinach and Feta Stuffed Chicken Breast slices on a platter. You can drizzle any pan juices over the top for extra flavor.

This Spinach and Feta Stuffed Chicken Breast is a flavorful and satisfying dish that's sure to impress. Enjoy!

15-Minute Beef and Vegetable Stir-Fry

Ingredients:

- 1 lb (450g) flank steak or sirloin, thinly sliced
- 2 tablespoons soy sauce
- 1 tablespoon oyster sauce
- 1 tablespoon hoisin sauce
- 1 tablespoon cornstarch
- 2 tablespoons vegetable oil, divided
- 3 cups mixed vegetables (broccoli florets, bell peppers, snap peas, carrots, etc.), chopped
- 3 cloves garlic, minced
- 1 teaspoon fresh ginger, grated
- 2 green onions, sliced (for garnish)
- Sesame seeds (optional, for garnish)
- Cooked rice or noodles for serving

Instructions:

Prepare the Beef:
- In a bowl, combine thinly sliced beef with soy sauce, oyster sauce, hoisin sauce, and cornstarch. Toss to coat the beef evenly and set aside for a few minutes.

Heat the Pan:
- Heat 1 tablespoon of vegetable oil in a wok or a large skillet over high heat.

Cook the Beef:
- Add the marinated beef to the hot pan, spreading it out to ensure even cooking. Cook for 2-3 minutes, stirring frequently, until the beef is browned and cooked through. Remove the beef from the pan and set it aside.

Cook the Vegetables:
- In the same pan, add another tablespoon of vegetable oil. Add minced garlic and grated ginger, sautéing for about 30 seconds until fragrant.
- Add the mixed vegetables to the pan and stir-fry for 3-4 minutes, or until they are tender-crisp.

Combine and Finish:

- Return the cooked beef to the pan with the vegetables. Toss everything together to combine and heat through.

Garnish and Serve:
- Garnish the stir-fry with sliced green onions and sesame seeds if desired.
- Serve the Beef and Vegetable Stir-Fry over cooked rice or noodles.

This 15-Minute Beef and Vegetable Stir-Fry is a quick and versatile dish. Feel free to customize it with your favorite vegetables and serve it with your preferred base. Enjoy your quick and tasty stir-fry!

Mango Coconut Chia Pudding Parfait

Ingredients:

For Mango Coconut Chia Pudding:

- 1/4 cup chia seeds
- 1 cup coconut milk
- 1 tablespoon maple syrup or honey
- 1 teaspoon vanilla extract
- 1 ripe mango, diced

For Parfait Assembly:

- Greek yogurt (or coconut yogurt for a dairy-free option)
- Fresh mango slices
- Toasted coconut flakes

Instructions:

In a bowl, mix together chia seeds, coconut milk, maple syrup (or honey), and vanilla extract. Stir well to combine.
Cover the bowl and refrigerate the chia pudding mixture for at least 4 hours or overnight, allowing it to thicken.
Once the chia pudding has reached a pudding-like consistency, stir it well to break up any clumps.
In serving glasses or bowls, layer the chia pudding with Greek yogurt.
Add a layer of diced mango on top of the yogurt.
Repeat the layers until you reach the top of the glass, finishing with a layer of mango.
Garnish with toasted coconut flakes for added flavor and texture.
Serve immediately and enjoy your Mango Coconut Chia Pudding Parfait!

Feel free to adjust the sweetness and thickness of the chia pudding according to your preferences. This refreshing parfait makes for a delightful and nutritious breakfast or dessert.

Sriracha Lime Grilled Shrimp Skewers

Ingredients:

- 1 pound large shrimp, peeled and deveined
- 3 tablespoons olive oil
- 2 tablespoons sriracha sauce (adjust to taste)
- Zest and juice of 2 limes
- 2 cloves garlic, minced
- 1 tablespoon honey
- 1 teaspoon soy sauce
- Salt and black pepper to taste
- Wooden or metal skewers, soaked if wooden

Instructions:

In a bowl, whisk together olive oil, sriracha sauce, lime zest, lime juice, minced garlic, honey, soy sauce, salt, and black pepper. This will be your marinade.
Place the shrimp in a resealable plastic bag or shallow dish and pour half of the marinade over them. Reserve the remaining marinade for basting and serving.
Toss the shrimp to coat evenly with the marinade. Seal the bag or cover the dish and let the shrimp marinate in the refrigerator for at least 30 minutes to allow the flavors to infuse.
Preheat your grill to medium-high heat.
Thread the marinated shrimp onto skewers, making sure to thread through both the tail and body of each shrimp.
Grill the shrimp skewers for 2-3 minutes per side or until they turn pink and opaque, basting with the reserved marinade during cooking.
Once the shrimp are cooked through, remove them from the grill and place on a serving platter.
Drizzle the skewers with any remaining marinade and serve immediately.

These Sriracha Lime Grilled Shrimp Skewers are perfect for a flavorful appetizer or a main course. Enjoy the combination of spicy sriracha, tangy lime, and succulent grilled shrimp!

Caprese Couscous Salad with Balsamic Vinaigrette

Ingredients:

For the Salad:

- 1 cup couscous
- 1 1/4 cups water or vegetable broth
- 1 pint cherry tomatoes, halved
- 8 ounces fresh mozzarella cheese, diced
- 1/2 cup fresh basil leaves, chopped
- Salt and black pepper to taste

For the Balsamic Vinaigrette:

- 1/4 cup balsamic vinegar
- 1/3 cup extra-virgin olive oil
- 1 teaspoon Dijon mustard
- 1 teaspoon honey
- 1 clove garlic, minced
- Salt and black pepper to taste

Instructions:

For the Salad:

In a medium saucepan, bring water or vegetable broth to a boil. Stir in the couscous, cover, and remove from heat. Let it sit for 5 minutes, then fluff with a fork.
Allow the couscous to cool to room temperature.
In a large bowl, combine the cooked couscous, cherry tomatoes, fresh mozzarella, and chopped basil.
Season the salad with salt and black pepper to taste. Toss gently to combine.

For the Balsamic Vinaigrette:

In a small bowl, whisk together balsamic vinegar, extra-virgin olive oil, Dijon mustard, honey, minced garlic, salt, and black pepper.
Taste the vinaigrette and adjust the seasonings if necessary.

Assembly:

Drizzle the prepared balsamic vinaigrette over the couscous salad.
Toss the salad gently to coat everything evenly with the vinaigrette.
Serve the Caprese Couscous Salad immediately, or refrigerate for a couple of hours to allow the flavors to meld.
Garnish with additional fresh basil leaves before serving, if desired.

This Caprese Couscous Salad with Balsamic Vinaigrette is a refreshing and flavorful dish that makes a great side or a light meal on its own. Enjoy the combination of couscous, juicy cherry tomatoes, creamy mozzarella, and aromatic basil!

Grilled Teriyaki Tofu and Pineapple Skewers

Ingredients:

For the Teriyaki Marinade:

- 1/4 cup soy sauce
- 2 tablespoons rice vinegar
- 2 tablespoons honey or maple syrup
- 1 tablespoon sesame oil
- 2 cloves garlic, minced
- 1 teaspoon ginger, grated
- 1 tablespoon cornstarch (optional, for thickening)

For the Skewers:

- 1 block extra-firm tofu, pressed and cut into cubes
- 1 cup pineapple chunks
- Bell peppers, cherry tomatoes, or other vegetables of choice
- Wooden or metal skewers, soaked if wooden

Instructions:

For the Teriyaki Marinade:

In a bowl, whisk together soy sauce, rice vinegar, honey (or maple syrup), sesame oil, minced garlic, and grated ginger.
If you prefer a thicker teriyaki sauce, mix in cornstarch. To do this, dissolve the cornstarch in a tablespoon of water and add it to the marinade. Whisk until well combined.

For the Skewers:

In a shallow dish, place the tofu cubes and pineapple chunks.
Pour half of the teriyaki marinade over the tofu and pineapple. Reserve the other half for basting and serving.

Marinate the tofu and pineapple for at least 30 minutes, allowing the flavors to absorb.

Preheat your grill or grill pan to medium-high heat.

Thread the marinated tofu, pineapple, and vegetables onto the skewers, alternating for a colorful presentation.

Grill the skewers for 3-4 minutes per side, basting with the reserved teriyaki marinade.

Continue grilling until the tofu is golden and has grill marks.

Once done, remove the skewers from the grill and place them on a serving platter.

Drizzle the skewers with any remaining teriyaki marinade and serve hot.

Enjoy these Grilled Teriyaki Tofu and Pineapple Skewers as a delicious and flavorful vegetarian option for your next barbecue or outdoor gathering!

Lemon Dill Salmon Salad Lettuce Wraps

Ingredients:

For the Salmon Salad:

- 1 pound cooked salmon, flaked
- 1/4 cup mayonnaise
- 1 tablespoon Dijon mustard
- Zest and juice of 1 lemon
- 2 tablespoons fresh dill, chopped
- Salt and black pepper to taste

For Lettuce Wraps:

- Large lettuce leaves (such as Bibb or Butter lettuce)

Optional Toppings:

- Sliced cucumber
- Cherry tomatoes, halved
- Avocado slices

Instructions:

For the Salmon Salad:

In a bowl, combine the flaked salmon, mayonnaise, Dijon mustard, lemon zest, lemon juice, and chopped dill.
Mix the ingredients together until well combined.
Season the salmon salad with salt and black pepper to taste. Adjust the seasoning if needed.

For Lettuce Wraps:

Wash and separate large lettuce leaves to create cups for the wraps.

Spoon a generous portion of the lemon dill salmon salad onto each lettuce leaf. Add optional toppings such as sliced cucumber, cherry tomatoes, and avocado. Serve immediately and enjoy!

These Lemon Dill Salmon Salad Lettuce Wraps make for a light and flavorful meal. They are perfect for a healthy lunch or dinner option. Feel free to customize the wraps with your favorite vegetables or herbs for added freshness and crunch.

Mediterranean Hummus and Veggie Wrap

Ingredients:

For the Hummus:

- 1 can (15 oz) chickpeas, drained and rinsed
- 3 tablespoons tahini
- 3 tablespoons extra-virgin olive oil
- 2 cloves garlic, minced
- Juice of 1 lemon
- 1 teaspoon ground cumin
- Salt and black pepper to taste
- Water (as needed to adjust consistency)

For the Wrap:

- Whole-grain or spinach tortillas
- 1 cup cherry tomatoes, halved
- 1 cucumber, thinly sliced
- 1 bell pepper (red or yellow), thinly sliced
- 1/2 red onion, thinly sliced
- Kalamata olives, pitted and sliced
- Feta cheese, crumbled
- Fresh parsley, chopped (for garnish)

Instructions:

For the Hummus:

In a food processor, combine chickpeas, tahini, olive oil, minced garlic, lemon juice, cumin, salt, and black pepper.
Blend the ingredients until smooth. If the hummus is too thick, add water gradually until you achieve your desired consistency.
Adjust seasoning to taste. Set aside.

For the Wrap:

Lay out the tortillas on a clean surface.

Spread a generous layer of the homemade hummus on each tortilla, leaving a border around the edges.

Layer the sliced cucumber, cherry tomatoes, bell pepper, red onion, olives, and crumbled feta cheese on top of the hummus.

Sprinkle fresh parsley over the veggies.

Fold in the sides of the tortilla and then roll it up tightly to create a wrap.

Repeat the process for the remaining wraps.

If desired, cut the wraps in half diagonally for easier handling.

Serve immediately and enjoy your Mediterranean Hummus and Veggie Wrap!

These wraps are not only delicious but also packed with Mediterranean flavors and plenty of fresh, colorful vegetables. They make a great lunch or light dinner option.